You're Not Alone, CHARLIE BROWN

by Charles M. Schulz

Selected Cartoons from
DON'T BE SAD, FLYING ACE and
CAN YOU BE MORE PACIFIC?

FAWCETT CREST • NEW YORK

A Fawcett Crest Book
Published by Ballantine Books
Copyright © 1990, 1991 by United Feature Syndicate, Inc.
PEANUTS Comic Strips © 1988 by United Feature Syndicate, Inc.

ISBN 0-449-22022-2

This book comprises portions of DON'T BE SAD, FLYING ACE and CAN YOU BE MORE PACIFIC? and is reprinted by arrangement with Pharos Books.

Manufactured in the United States of America

First Ballantine Books Edition: October 1992

All the Answers
(AND MUCH MUCH MORE)

You're Not Alone, CHARLIE BROWN

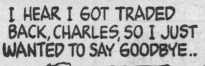

FOR "SHOW AND TELL" TODAY, I HAVE BROUGHT MY NEW "PRAYING DOLL"

YOU WILL NOTE THAT HER HANDS ARE HELD TOGETHER IN A PRAYING POSITION BY VELCRO..ARE THERE ANY QUESTIONS?

NO, I DO NOT BELIEVE VELCRO IS MENTIONED ANY-WHERE IN THE NEW TESTAMENT

SCHULZ

WELL, HOW WAS THE KITE-FLYING?

I HATE TO ADMIT IT, BUT I JUST SAW SOMETHING THAT MADE ME FEEL REAL GOOD..

3-27

IT SAYS HERE THEY'RE SERVING SHERBET AFTER THE CONCERT...

NO, IT SAYS THEY'RE PLAYING SCHUBERT DURING THE CONCERT..

3-31

FOR A MINUTE THERE I WAS GLAD I CAME

YOU'RE WEIRD, SIR!

SORRY, BUT IT'S HARD TO HIT 'EM RIGHT TO YOU..

PEANUTS.

by
SCHULZ

VOL. 2

DOES MONSIEUR FLYING ACE KNOW THAT NEXT WEEK IS THE BIRTHDAY OF THE RED BARON?

SHE'S RIGHT.. I SHOULD SEND HIM A CARD... SOMETHING SENTIMENTAL..

LIKE, "HAVE A NICE DAY"

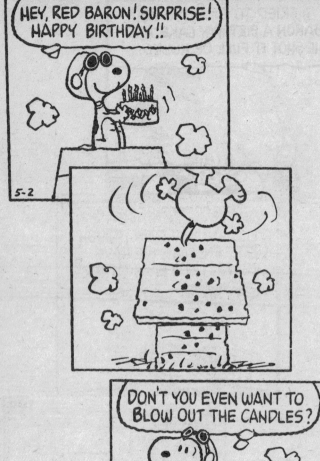

I TRIED TO GIVE THE RED BARON A BIRTHDAY CAKE, AND HE SHOT IT FULL OF HOLES...

JE REGRETTE BEAUCOUP.. DON'T BE SAD, FLYING ACE... YOU WERE VERY BRAVE, AND YOU MADE HIM LOOK FOOLISH..

5-3

TOUT VA BIEN! SOMEDAY THEY WILL LAUGH AND SAY, "HE SHOT DOWN EIGHTY PLANES AND ONE BIRTHDAY CAKE!"

OUR TEACHER WANTS US TO WRITE AN ESSAY ON PRAYING..

PRAYING IS IMPORTANT WHEN YOU WAKE UP AT TWO O'CLOCK IN THE MORNING FEELING SICK FROM EATING SOMETHING DUMB THE DAY BEFORE..

I'LL JUST SAY WE WERE OUT OF TOWN AND I DIDN'T HAVE TIME TO WRITE ANYTHING..

5-5

THE ANNUAL BUSINESS MEETING OF THE CACTUS CLUB WILL COME TO ORDER..

THE BUILDING COMMITTEE REPORTS THAT THE BANK WILL NOT BE LOANING US FIFTY MILLION DOLLARS TO BUILD A NEW CLUBHOUSE..

5-7

MAINLY BECAUSE I DIDN'T HAVE THE NERVE TO ASK ...

SCHULZ

PEANUTS.

by SCHULZ

I'VE DECIDED TO START EATING MORE VEGETABLES FOR LUNCH..

5-13

CARROT CAKE IS NOT A VEGETABLE..

SCHULZ

KEEP THE
BALL LOW

5-14

PEANUTS.

by SCHULZ

WHEN MY GRAMPA WALKS THROUGH THE PARKING LOT AT THE MALL, HE ALWAYS WALKS LIKE HE'S REAL COOL

WHY DOES HE WALK LIKE HE'S REAL COOL?

SO NO ONE WILL KNOW THAT HE'S FORGOTTEN WHERE HE PARKED HIS CAR!

5-20

PEANUTS.

by SCHULZ

" DEAR STUDENT, AS PART OF A STATEWIDE SCHOOL PROJECT, WE ARE ASKING WHAT YOU ARE READING NOW "

5-21

Right now, I am reading your form letter.

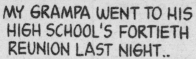

MY GRAMPA WENT TO HIS HIGH SCHOOL'S FORTIETH REUNION LAST NIGHT..

HE'S ALSO BEEN TO A COLLEGE REUNION AND AN ARMY REUNION...

5-25

HE HAS A NEW CAREER.. HE GOES BACK TO THINGS

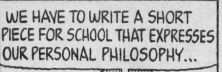

WE HAVE TO WRITE A SHORT PIECE FOR SCHOOL THAT EXPRESSES OUR PERSONAL PHILOSOPHY...

SO FAR I'VE WRITTEN, "WHO CARES?" AND "FORGET IT!"

HOW ABOUT "WHY ME?"

THAT'S GOOD.. I'LL FIT IT IN

PEANUTS

by SCHULZ

5-30

PEANUTS.

by SCHULZ

NOW THAT YOUR GRAMPA IS RETIRED, HOW DOES HE SPEND HIS TIME?

HE SAYS HE'S BUSY ALL DAY..

6-3

DOING WHAT?

GRAMPA THINGS..

HEY, PITCHER! IT HURTS MY NECK WATCHING THE OTHER TEAM HIT HOME RUNS OVER MY HEAD!

MAYBE I'LL JUST FACE THE OTHER WAY, AND THEN I WON'T HAVE TO TURN AROUND EVERY TIME...YES, THIS IS GOING TO BE MUCH BETTER..

6-4

IT'S A NICE FEELING KNOWING THAT YOUR PLAYERS ARE COMFORTABLE

PEANUTS.

by SCHULZ

MY DOG HAS GONE TO NEEDLES TO SELL SOUVENIRS AT THE OLYMPIC GAMES..

THAT STUPID DOG! HOW WILL HE KNOW WHICH WAY TO GO?

LET'S SEE NOW..NEEDLES IS IN THE WEST..THE MOON IS ALWAYS OVER HOLLYWOOD, AND HOLLYWOOD IS IN THE WEST..SO...

6-11

SCHULZ

PEANUTS.

by SCHULZ

WHY DO I RUSH DOWN HERE EVERY MORNING TEN MINUTES AHEAD OF TIME SO I WON'T MISS THE SCHOOL BUS?

BUS

..AND THEN STAND HERE FOR TEN MINUTES HOPING IT WON'T COME?

12-5

BUS

PEANUTS.

by SCHULZ

MY BROTHER HAS GONE BACK HOME BECAUSE HE SAID I SHOULDN'T HAVE BEEN LISTENING TO A CACTUS

WHO ELSE CAN I LISTEN TO? WHO ELSE CAN I TALK TO?

6-25

PEANUTS.

by SCHULZ

THAT COMPOSER HAD A TRAGIC LIFE, DIDN'T HE?

BUT IT WAS ROMANTIC

6-28

ROMANTIC?

A TRAGIC LIFE IS ROMANTIC WHEN IT HAPPENS TO SOMEBODY ELSE..

I WOKE UP LAST NIGHT BITING MY TONGUE..

I USED TO DO THAT WHEN I WAS A PUPPY.. IT REALLY HURTS...

BUT NOT AS BAD AS STEPPING ON YOUR EARS..

SCHULZ   7-5

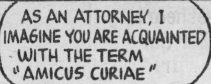

7-13 SCHULZ

CHARLIE BROWN, SNOOPY
and the whole **PEANUTS**® gang...

Copr. © 1952
United Feature Syndicate, Inc.

together again with another set of
daily trials and tribulations by

CHARLES M. SCHULZ